COLE M. GABRIEL

The Life Of Saint Frances of Rome

Copyright © 2024 by Cole M. Gabriel

All rights reserved. No part of this publication may be reproduced, stored or transmitted in any form or by any means, electronic, mechanical, photocopying, recording, scanning, or otherwise without written permission from the publisher. It is illegal to copy this book, post it to a website, or distribute it by any other means without permission.

First edition

*This book was professionally typeset on Reedsy.
Find out more at reedsy.com*

Contents

Preface		iv
1	Early Life	1
2	Marriage And Family	4
3	Spiritual Awakening	7
4	Charitable Works	10
5	Life Of Humility	13
6	Devotion To The Eucharist	17
7	Miracles And Mystical Experiences	22
8	Legacy	26
9	Devotions To Saint Frances Of Rome	31
10	Conclusion	53

Preface

Saint Frances of Rome, a luminary in the tapestry of Catholic saints, graced the world in the year 1384. Her life, spanning the late medieval period, unfolded against the backdrop of societal norms and ecclesiastical fervor. Born into Italian nobility, Frances navigated the intricate dance of privilege and responsibility from an early age. This introduction peels back the layers of her remarkable journey, exploring the multifaceted facets that shaped her into an exemplar of piety and charity.

In an era where arranged marriages were the norm, Frances found herself entwined in the threads of matrimony. Her union, initially a societal expectation, became a crucible for the forging of her character. The contours of her family life and the responsibilities that accompanied her station offered her a canvas upon which she painted the colors of humility and compassion.

Yet, it was within the crucible of her own spiritual awakening that Frances truly discovered her life's purpose. Moments of divine revelation and influences on her faith propelled her beyond the confines of her noble status. The stirrings of a profound spirituality ignited within her a fervent desire to serve the marginalized and downtrodden.

The founding of the Oblates of Mary stands as a testament to Frances' commitment to the service of the poor and sick. The order, a manifestation of her compassionate vision, sought to alleviate suffering and bring solace to those on the fringes of society. Frances, though born into opulence, embraced a life of simplicity, choosing to personally minister to those in need, shattering societal expectations with every selfless act.

At the heart of her devotion was an unwavering commitment to the Eucharist. The significance of this sacrament in her life became a guiding force, influencing her practices and rituals. Her profound connection with the Eucharist not only anchored her spirituality but also became a source of inspiration for those who witnessed her devotion.

Miracles and mystical experiences punctuated Frances' earthly journey, adding an ethereal dimension to her narrative. Reported miracles and mystical encounters became part of the tapestry of her saintly existence, further solidifying her place in the celestial realm.

Canonized in 1608, Saint Frances of Rome's legacy extends far beyond the confines of her temporal existence. Her life continues to inspire, a testament to the enduring power of selflessness, faith, and compassion. As we embark on this exploration of her life, we unravel the threads of a saint who, against the backdrop of medieval Italy, emerged as a beacon of light, reminding us of the transformative potential of a life lived in service to others.

1

Early Life

Born in the year 1384 in Rome, Italy, Saint Frances of Rome entered the world into a noble family, her lineage intertwining with the fabric of Italian aristocracy. Her parents, Paul Bussa and Jacobella dei Roffredeschi, belonged to the upper echelons of society, providing Frances with a privileged upbringing that was characteristic of her time.

Frances' early years unfolded within the confines of her family's prestigious residence, where the air was permeated with the influence of nobility and the trappings of privilege. The cultural and societal milieu in which she was raised shaped her perceptions of the world, setting the stage for the unconventional path she would later tread.

As a member of the nobility, Frances was afforded the luxury of education, a rarity for women in medieval society. Her family's affluence enabled her to receive an education that extended beyond the domestic sphere, contributing to the intellectual foundation that would later inform her spiritual journey.

The intricacies of Frances' familial relationships played a crucial role in shaping her character. The dynamics within the household, the expectations placed upon her as a daughter, and the values instilled by her parents all contributed to the formation of her identity. These early familial influences, while steeped in the traditions of the aristocracy, would eventually collide with the currents of Frances' profound spiritual awakening, setting her on a course that diverged from the path expected of a woman of her station.

Frances of Rome's upbringing was a tapestry woven with the threads of nobility and privilege. Raised within the opulent confines of her family's residence in 14th-century Rome, she experienced a childhood colored by the refined tastes and cultural influences characteristic of Italian aristocracy.

Her upbringing was not only defined by material abundance but also by the societal expectations that accompanied her noble status. Frances, as a young girl, navigated the delicate balance between fulfilling the roles prescribed for a daughter of her station and the stirrings of her individual spirit.

In a departure from the norms of the time, Frances received an education that extended beyond the confines of domesticity. Her family's affluence afforded her the rare opportunity to engage with intellectual pursuits, a privilege not commonly extended to women during the medieval period. This educational foundation laid the groundwork for a woman whose later life would be marked by a blend of worldly wisdom and spiritual depth.

EARLY LIFE

The influences of her upbringing, both the privileges and constraints, played a pivotal role in shaping Frances' character. The refined tastes and cultural exposures of her aristocratic environment juxtaposed with the societal expectations placed upon her as a young woman of noble birth. These early experiences would prove to be instrumental in the unfolding of Frances' unconventional path, one that would see her transcend the confines of societal norms and carve a unique niche in the history of Catholic sanctity.

2

Marriage And Family

Frances of Rome's life took a significant turn with the arrangement of her marriage, a common practice in the social fabric of medieval Italy. In accordance with the customs of the time, Frances, at the age of 12, found herself betrothed to Lorenzo Ponziani, a young nobleman from a respected Roman family.

The union, orchestrated by their respective families, was not solely a matter of personal choice but rather a strategic alliance designed to strengthen familial ties and consolidate social standing. Despite the transactional nature of such arrangements, Frances approached her marital duties with a sense of commitment, navigating the complexities of her new role as a wife with a blend of grace and resilience.

The challenges and responsibilities of married life did not deter Frances from her innate sense of compassion and charity. Even within the confines of her marital duties, she began to weave the threads of her spiritual journey, laying the foundation for a life that would extend beyond the conventional roles expected of a woman in her societal position.

Frances' marriage, though rooted in tradition and societal expectations, became a crucible for the forging of her character. It set the stage for a woman whose resilience, devotion, and eventual transformation would transcend the boundaries imposed by her arranged union, propelling her towards a higher calling—one that would redefine the purpose of her existence and leave an indelible mark on the pages of Catholic hagiography.

Within the confines of her arranged marriage to Lorenzo Ponziani, Frances of Rome navigated the intricate tapestry of family life and responsibilities. As the wife of a nobleman in 14th-century Italy, her days were woven with the threads of societal expectations, yet she approached her roles with a unique blend of grace and purpose.

Frances bore the responsibilities inherent in her station with diligence, managing the affairs of her household and attending to the needs of her family. Her days were filled with the demands of maintaining a noble residence, overseeing domestic matters, and participating in the social rituals expected of someone of her status.

Despite the societal norms that dictated the roles of women in her time, Frances infused her family life with a spirit of compassion. Her innate sense of charity extended beyond the walls of her home, as she sought to alleviate the suffering of those less fortunate. This inclination towards charity and empathy would later become a defining aspect of her saintly legacy.

The dynamics within her family, the interactions with her husband Lorenzo, and the bonds formed with her children provided the backdrop against which Frances' spirituality evolved. Her commitment to familial duties did not hinder her from exploring the deeper dimensions of her faith, setting the stage for a remarkable journey that would eventually lead her to a life dedicated to serving others.

In the crucible of family life, Frances of Rome forged the foundation of her character, laying the groundwork for a transformative path that would transcend the confines of societal expectations and redefine the purpose of her existence.

3

Spiritual Awakening

Frances of Rome's spiritual journey was marked by profound moments of awakening, stirring within her a devotion that transcended the confines of societal expectations. Amidst the backdrop of her noble existence, these transformative moments became the catalysts for her deepening faith.

One such pivotal moment occurred during a pilgrimage to the tombs of the apostles in Rome. As Frances knelt in prayer, she experienced a profound spiritual revelation, sensing a calling beyond the trappings of her aristocratic life. This encounter became a cornerstone in her journey, sparking a desire to explore the depths of her faith and cultivate a more intimate connection with the divine.

Another significant moment unfolded during a time of personal distress when Frances faced the loss of her children and other familial challenges. In the crucible of grief, she turned to her faith for solace and guidance. It was within these trials that her spirituality matured, leading her to embrace a life of greater purpose and service.

These moments of spiritual awakening were not isolated occurrences but rather a series of encounters that gradually transformed Frances' perspective. Her growing awareness of the impermanence of worldly pursuits fueled a desire for a more profound connection with God, propelling her towards a life dedicated to charity and selfless service.

Frances of Rome's spiritual awakening, intertwined with the fabric of her personal trials and moments of divine revelation, laid the foundation for the extraordinary path she would embark upon—a path guided by faith, compassion, and an unwavering commitment to a higher calling.

Frances of Rome's faith was shaped by a confluence of influences that spanned both personal experiences and external factors, contributing to the depth and richness of her spiritual journey.

Frances embarked on pilgrimages, including visits to the tombs of the apostles in Rome. These sacred journeys provided her with a tangible connection to the roots of Christianity, fostering a sense of reverence and deepening her understanding of the faith.

As a woman of the nobility, Frances had access to ecclesiastical teachings and guidance. The theological foundation laid by the Church played a significant role in shaping her beliefs and understanding of Christian doctrine.

The challenges she faced, including the loss of her children, served as crucibles for spiritual growth. Amidst personal grief, Frances found solace in her faith, leading her to seek a more profound understanding of God's plan for her life.

Frances surrounded herself with like-minded individuals, including spiritual mentors and companions. The exchange of ideas, shared prayers, and communal devotion provided her with a supportive environment that nurtured her evolving spirituality.

Engaging in contemplative practices, such as prayer and meditation, played a crucial role in deepening Frances' connection with the divine. These moments of introspection allowed her to cultivate a more intimate relationship with God.

The stark contrast between her privileged life and the plight of the less fortunate fueled Frances' sense of social justice. Her encounters with the suffering of the poor and sick prompted her to align her faith with acts of charity and service.

Frances reported mystical experiences and encounters with the divine. These moments of revelation further fueled her spiritual journey, reinforcing her conviction and providing a transcendent dimension to her faith.

In the tapestry of Frances of Rome's faith, these influences interwove to create a nuanced and deeply personal spirituality. Her journey stands as a testament to the transformative power of diverse influences converging to shape a person's relationship with the divine.

4

Charitable Works

Frances of Rome's profound spiritual journey culminated in the establishment of the Oblates of Mary, a lay order dedicated to serving the poor and sick. This pivotal moment in her life marked a departure from societal expectations and a radical commitment to a life of charity and compassion.

Inspired by her encounters with the suffering of the less fortunate, Frances, along with other like-minded individuals, founded the Oblates of Mary in 1425. This lay association sought to emulate the spirit of the early Christian community, where individuals shared their resources and lives in service to others.

The Oblates of Mary embraced a unique blend of contemplative and active spirituality. Members, though living in the world, committed themselves to a rule of life that included prayer, simplicity, and service. Frances, despite her noble background, actively participated in the daily activities of the order, personally ministering to the sick and destitute.

CHARITABLE WORKS

The establishment of the Oblates of Mary reflected Frances' unwavering commitment to translating her faith into tangible acts of love and mercy. The order quickly gained recognition for its charitable endeavors, becoming a beacon of hope for the marginalized in medieval Rome.

Frances' vision for the Oblates of Mary was not just a charitable initiative but a transformative way of life one that challenged the prevailing norms and exemplified a radical commitment to Christian virtues. The order's existence became a testament to Frances of Rome's enduring legacy, inspiring generations to follow in the path of selfless service and devotion to the less fortunate.

Frances of Rome's dedication to serving the poor and sick was the heartbeat of her saintly mission. Motivated by a deep sense of compassion and a profound understanding of Christian charity, she personally engaged in acts of mercy that went beyond societal expectations.

Frances actively ventured into the impoverished areas of Rome, reaching out to those in need. Her personal encounters with the destitute were characterized by humility and a hands-on approach, as she personally attended to the sick and comforted the suffering.

Recognizing the systemic nature of poverty and illness, Frances played a pivotal role in establishing hospitals and shelters for the marginalized. These institutions became havens for those without resources, providing not only physical care but also a sense of dignity.

In addition to addressing immediate physical needs, Frances provided material and spiritual support to the poor. Whether it was distributing alms, offering food and clothing, or sharing words of encouragement, her acts of charity were holistic and aimed at uplifting both body and spirit.

The lay order she co-founded, the Oblates of Mary, became an instrumental vehicle for her mission. Members of the order actively participated in serving the poor and sick, extending the reach and impact of Frances' compassionate initiatives.

Frances, despite her noble background, embraced a lifestyle of personal sacrifice. She divested herself of luxuries to be more attuned to the needs of the less fortunate. This commitment to simplicity and self-denial reflected her profound understanding of solidarity with the poor.

Beyond physical care, Frances offered spiritual consolation to those she served. Her presence provided solace to the sick and comfort to the downtrodden, emphasizing the holistic nature of her mission to alleviate both physical and spiritual suffering.

Frances of Rome's tireless efforts to serve the poor and sick exemplify the transformative power of personal commitment and love in the face of human suffering. Her legacy continues to inspire a legacy of compassion, urging others to follow in her footsteps of selfless service.

5

Life Of Humility

Frances of Rome, despite her noble birth and the societal expectations of her time, embraced a simple lifestyle that spoke volumes about her commitment to humility and spiritual values.

Frances chose to dress modestly, eschewing the luxurious clothing associated with her aristocratic status. Her attire reflected a deliberate choice to distance herself from material excess and align her life with the principles of simplicity.

Her residence, once a symbol of aristocratic opulence, underwent a transformation. Frances adopted a lifestyle of austerity, forgoing unnecessary luxuries in her living quarters. This intentional simplicity became a visible expression of her desire to detach from worldly comforts.

Frances willingly made personal sacrifices, divesting herself of material wealth to live a life more attuned to the needs of the less fortunate. This conscious choice to embrace self-denial exemplified her dedication to a lifestyle that prioritized others over personal comfort.

Fasting and abstaining from indulgences were integral aspects of Frances' simple lifestyle. These practices were not mere rituals but expressions of her commitment to spiritual discipline and a reminder of the transience of worldly pleasures.

Her daily life centered around meeting essential needs rather than indulging in excess. By simplifying her material desires, Frances redirected her resources and attention toward the service of others, particularly the poor and sick.

The lay order she co-founded, the Oblates of Mary, also embraced a lifestyle of simplicity. Members of the order followed a rule of life that echoed Frances' commitment to humility and self-denial, fostering a communal ethos of shared simplicity.

Frances of Rome's embrace of a simple lifestyle was not a renunciation of her past but a conscious choice to align her life with the teachings of Christ. Her example continues to resonate, challenging individuals to reconsider societal norms and embrace a life marked by humility, compassion, and a focus on what truly matters.

Frances of Rome's life was characterized by a series of profound personal sacrifices, each undertaken with the singular aim of serving others and living out her commitment to Christian charity.

1. Wealth Redistribution:

Frances willingly redistributed her wealth, divesting herself of material luxuries to alleviate the suffering of the less fortunate. Her personal sacrifices were not symbolic but tangible, reflecting a commitment to share resources with those in need.

2. Living Modestly:

Despite her noble background, Frances chose to live modestly, forgoing the trappings of aristocratic opulence. This intentional simplicity in her lifestyle allowed her to identify with the poor and create a space where material excess did not overshadow her mission of service.

3. Hands-On Care for the Sick:

Frances personally attended to the sick, administering care and comfort with her own hands. Her willingness to immerse herself in the physical needs of the suffering demonstrated a profound level of personal sacrifice for the well-being of others.

4. Time and Presence:

Frances sacrificially dedicated her time and presence to those she served. Her availability to those in need went beyond mere gestures, as she actively engaged in personal interactions, offering solace and companionship to the lonely and distressed.

5. Establishing Hospitals:

The establishment of hospitals for the sick was a monumental personal sacrifice. Frances invested not only her financial resources but also her time and energy in creating institutions that provided comprehensive care for the afflicted.

6. Fasting for Others:

Frances incorporated fasting and abstinence into her spiritual discipline, not as a personal ascetic practice, but as a form of intercession for the needs of others. Her self-imposed sacrifices were a spiritual offering for the well-being of the community.

7. Simplicity in Personal Comfort:

Her personal comfort took a back seat to the needs of others. Frances' deliberate choice to live with simplicity and humility underscored her commitment to prioritizing the well-being of those who lacked the privileges she once enjoyed.

Frances of Rome's personal sacrifices were not acts of self-flagellation but deliberate choices rooted in a profound understanding of Christian love and service. Her life remains a testament to the transformative power of sacrificial living, inspiring generations to emulate her example in the pursuit of a more compassionate and selfless existence.

6

Devotion To The Eucharist

The Eucharist held profound significance in the life of Frances of Rome, serving as a cornerstone of her spirituality and a source of transformative grace.

For Frances, the Eucharist was a sacred communion with the divine. Partaking in the Body and Blood of Christ during the Mass was not a mere ritual but a deeply personal encounter that nourished her soul and strengthened her connection with God.

The regular reception of the Eucharist became the foundation of Frances' spiritual strength. The grace she believed emanated from the sacrament empowered her to navigate the challenges of her noble life, personal losses, and the demanding work of serving the poor and sick.

During moments of personal trial and sorrow, the Eucharist served as a guiding light. Frances found solace and resilience in the presence of Christ, drawing strength from the sacrament to face the adversities in her life, including the loss of her children.

The Eucharist inspired Frances to translate her faith into tangible acts of charity. The selfless love exemplified in the sacrament fueled her desire to emulate Christ's compassion, motivating her to serve the less fortunate and establish the Oblates of Mary.

Frances seamlessly integrated her worship through the Eucharist with her commitment to serving others. Her acts of charity were an extension of her participation in the sacrificial meal, exemplifying the inseparable connection between the spiritual and the practical aspects of her life.

Beyond the Mass, Frances engaged in Eucharistic adoration, spending devoted time in prayer before the Blessed Sacrament. This contemplative practice deepened her intimacy with Christ and further fueled her dedication to a life of charity.

The significance of the Eucharist in Frances' life became a model for the Oblates of Mary. The lay order she co-founded embraced the sacrament as a central element of their spiritual life, reinforcing the transformative impact of the Eucharist on their charitable mission.

Frances of Rome's devotion to the Eucharist was not a mere ritualistic observance but a dynamic and transformative encounter with the divine. The sacrament served as a wellspring of spiritual nourishment, fortifying her in her journey of faith, service, and selfless love.

Frances of Rome's life was characterized by a set of practices and rituals that were deeply rooted in her spirituality, guiding her daily existence and shaping her path of service and devotion.

1. Daily Prayer:

A cornerstone of Frances' life was a disciplined practice of daily prayer. She devoted specific times to communion with God, seeking guidance, strength, and gratitude through intimate conversations with the divine.

2. Eucharistic Participation:

Regular participation in the Eucharistic celebration was a central ritual for Frances. Attending Mass, partaking in the sacrament, and engaging in Eucharistic adoration were not just routine practices but vital moments of communion with Christ.

3. Contemplative Reflection:

Frances incorporated contemplative reflection into her daily routine. Moments of silence and introspection allowed her to deepen her connection with God, fostering a sense of spiritual awareness and discernment in the midst of her active life.

4. Fasting and Abstinence:

Fasting and abstaining from certain indulgences were integral aspects of Frances' spiritual discipline. These practices were not undertaken for mere asceticism but were expressions of self-control and solidarity with the suffering of Christ.

5. Works of Charity:

Acts of charity and service were daily rituals for Frances. Whether personally attending to the sick, distributing alms, or establishing hospitals, her commitment to serving others became a lived expression of her faith.

6. Liturgical Seasons Observance:

Frances observed the liturgical seasons with reverence. The cycles of the Church calendar shaped her spiritual practices, allowing her to engage more deeply with the mysteries of the Christian faith and align her life with the rhythm of the liturgical year.

7. Rule of Life for the Oblates of Mary:

As co-founder of the Oblates of Mary, Frances established a rule of life for the members. This set of practices and rituals guided the daily activities of the lay order, emphasizing prayer, simplicity, and service as integral components of their shared spirituality.

8. Visiting Sacred Sites:

Pilgrimages to sacred sites held significance for Frances. Visits to holy places and shrines allowed her to deepen her connection with the Christian tradition, providing opportunities for reflection, prayer, and renewal of spiritual commitment.

9. Acts of Penitence:

Acknowledging human imperfection, Frances incorporated acts of penitence into her spiritual life. Confession, contrition, and a commitment to continuous personal improvement were integral components of her journey towards holiness.

These practices and rituals formed a tapestry of devotion for Frances of Rome, shaping her into a saint whose daily life was a seamless integration of contemplation, service, and a profound commitment to living out the teachings of her faith.

7

Miracles And Mystical Experiences

While there are no specific, widely reported miracles directly associated with Frances of Rome, her life is nonetheless surrounded by a spiritual aura that includes instances of divine favor and intercession attributed to her. In the context of canonization and sainthood, the Catholic Church often investigates reports of miracles to affirm a candidate's sanctity.

1. Healing Miracles:

There are accounts of individuals attributing their healing to the intercession of Frances of Rome. These healing miracles often involve ailments or illnesses for which individuals sought her spiritual assistance through prayer.

2. Protection from Perils:

Some followers have reported instances where they believe Frances interceded to protect them from harm or imminent dangers. These anecdotes highlight a sense of divine intervention associated with her spiritual presence.

3. Multiplication of Resources:

Stories exist of Frances aiding the poor and destitute, where meager resources were miraculously multiplied to meet the needs of a greater number. These instances are often seen as a manifestation of divine providence through her intercession.

4. Answers to Prayer:

Devotees attribute answered prayers to Frances of Rome. Whether seeking guidance, solace, or assistance in times of need, individuals have reported experiencing what they perceive as direct responses to their prayers through her intercession.

5. Posthumous Miracles:

After her death, some followers claim to have witnessed posthumous miracles associated with relics or objects connected to Frances. These reports often include accounts of healing or other extraordinary events attributed to her spiritual presence.

It's essential to note that the recognition of miracles in the context of canonization follows a rigorous process by the Catholic Church. These reported miracles are subject to thorough investigation and scrutiny by ecclesiastical authorities before any official acknowledgment is made. While the specific miracles associated with Frances of Rome might not be as widely documented as those of some other saints, her spiritual influence is acknowledged through the veneration and devotion of those who believe in her intercession.

Frances of Rome's spiritual journey was enriched by mystical encounters and visions, which she reportedly experienced during moments of deep prayer and contemplation.

Frances is said to have received divine locutions direct communications from God while in prayer. These moments of inner revelation were deeply personal and contributed to the shaping of her spiritual understanding and mission.

Accounts suggest that Frances had visions of guardian angels. These celestial beings were believed to guide and protect her on her spiritual journey, offering both comfort and divine guidance.

In moments of profound prayer, Frances reported experiencing a mystical unity with Christ. These experiences of spiritual union are often described in mystical literature as a profound sense of being one with the divine.

Frances had intense visions of the Passion of Christ. These mystical encounters allowed her to enter deeply into the suffering of Christ, fostering a profound sense of empathy and solidarity with the redemptive aspects of Christ's sacrifice.

Given her deep devotion to the Eucharist, Frances is said to have had mystical visions related to this sacrament. These visions may have included a heightened perception of the sacredness of the Eucharistic elements and a profound understanding of their spiritual significance.

Mystical encounters with God also reportedly granted Frances prophetic insights. These revelations about future events or spiritual truths were seen as a manifestation of divine knowledge communicated to her in moments of deep communion with the divine.

Frances claimed to receive guidance and spiritual companionship from Saint Agnes, a fellow Roman saint. This mystical connection with another saint added a layer of spiritual richness to her experiences.

At times, Frances of Rome entered states of transcendent ecstasy during prayer. These mystical ecstasies were moments of profound spiritual joy and union with the divine, lifting her beyond the constraints of the material world.

It's important to recognize that mystical encounters and visions are deeply personal experiences, often challenging to convey in concrete terms. While these aspects of Frances of Rome's life are reported in hagiographical accounts, they are received with a certain degree of faith and reverence within the context of her spiritual journey.

8

Legacy

Saint Frances of Rome was canonized by Pope Paul V on May 29, 1608, nearly two centuries after her death in 1440. The process of canonization involves a thorough investigation into the life, virtues, and reported miracles of a candidate for sainthood.

1. Beatification:

Frances' journey toward sainthood began with her beatification, a declaration by the Catholic Church that she lived a life of heroic virtue. Pope Leo X beatified her on November 9, 1608, recognizing her sanctity and the exemplary nature of her Christian life.

2. Canonization:

After beatification, the Church undertakes a meticulous examination of the candidate's life, writings, and the reported miracles attributed to their intercession. In the case of Frances of Rome, her canonization took place on May 29, 1608, confirming her status as a saint in the Catholic Church.

3. Process of Canonization:

The canonization process involves several stages, including the appointment of a postulator to present the case for sainthood, the collection of evidence supporting the candidate's virtues and miracles, and a thorough examination by theologians and cardinals.

4. Miracles:

The recognition of miracles attributed to the intercession of the candidate is a crucial aspect of canonization. In Frances' case, reported miracles, often involving healing, were scrutinized and accepted as evidence of her ongoing intercessory power.

5. Papal Decree:

The final step in the canonization process is the papal decree issued by the Pope, officially declaring the candidate a saint. In the case of Saint Frances of Rome, Pope Paul V issued the decree on May 29, 1608, formally acknowledging her holiness and placing her in the canon of saints.

6. Feast Day:

Upon canonization, a saint is assigned a feast day in the liturgical calendar. Saint Frances of Rome is commemorated on March 9, the date of her death, as a day to celebrate her life, virtue, and contributions to the Church.

Saint Frances of Rome is revered for her deep spirituality, commitment to charity, and the transformative impact of her life. Her canonization is a testament to the recognition by the Catholic Church of her sanctity and the enduring influence of her example in the lives of believers.

The continued influence of Saint Frances of Rome extends beyond her canonization, resonating in various ways within the Catholic Church and inspiring individuals in their spiritual journeys.

1. Devotion and Veneration:
Devotion to Saint Frances of Rome persists among the faithful. Many continue to venerate her as a model of Christian virtue, turning to her in prayer for intercession, guidance, and inspiration in their daily lives.

2. Oblates of Saint Frances of Rome:
The lay order she co-founded, the Oblates of Saint Frances of Rome, continues to exist as a living legacy of her commitment to serving the poor and sick. The members, inspired by her example, carry on her mission, dedicating their lives to acts of charity and compassion.

3. Charitable Works:
Frances' emphasis on charitable works has left an enduring impact on Catholic charitable organizations and individuals engaged in acts of mercy. Her legacy serves as a reminder of the transformative power of selfless service to the less fortunate.

4. Patron Saint:
Saint Frances of Rome is recognized as the patron saint

of numerous causes, including widows, against the death of children, and automobile drivers. People invoke her intercession for protection, guidance, and assistance in various aspects of their lives.

5. Artistic and Cultural Depictions:

The life of Saint Frances of Rome has been depicted in art, literature, and religious iconography. These representations serve to commemorate her sanctity and convey her story to future generations.

6. Feast Day Celebrations:

March 9, the feast day of Saint Frances of Rome, is commemorated with special liturgical celebrations and devotions in the Catholic Church. This annual event allows believers to reflect on her life and contributions to the Church.

7. Spiritual Retreats and Pilgrimages:

Pilgrims and individuals seeking spiritual enrichment often visit places associated with Saint Frances of Rome. Spiritual retreats and pilgrimages to sites significant in her life provide opportunities for deeper connection with her legacy.

8. Educational and Inspirational Resources:

Books, articles, and educational materials continue to be produced about Saint Frances of Rome, disseminating her story and teachings. These resources serve as a source of inspiration for those seeking to incorporate her virtues into their own lives.

The continued influence and commemoration of Saint Frances of Rome underscore the enduring impact of her life on the spiritual landscape. Through the ongoing devotion of the faithful and the perpetuation of her legacy, she remains a guiding figure, inspiring individuals to live lives of faith, charity, and compassion.

9

Devotions To Saint Frances Of Rome

Devotion to Saint Frances of Rome is characterized by a deep and enduring reverence for her life, virtues, and spiritual teachings. Believers turn to her as a source of inspiration, guidance, and intercession, seeking to emulate her exemplary Christian virtues.

1. Prayer and Intercession:

Devotees of Saint Frances of Rome often turn to her in prayer, seeking her intercession in times of need or for specific intentions. They believe that her sanctity and closeness to God make her a powerful advocate in heaven.

2. Mimicking Her Virtues:

Those devoted to Saint Frances strive to incorporate her virtues into their own lives. Whether it's practicing charity, humility, or self-sacrifice, believers see her as a model of Christian virtue and seek to mirror her qualities in their daily actions.

3. Feast Day Celebrations:

March 9, the feast day of Saint Frances of Rome, is a special occasion for devotion. Believers commemorate her life through liturgical celebrations, prayer services, and reflections on her contributions to the Church.

4. Establishment of Devotional Groups:

Some communities or parishes may form devotional groups or societies dedicated to Saint Frances of Rome. These groups provide a platform for collective prayer, reflection, and the sharing of experiences related to devotion to the saint.

5. Pilgrimages to Holy Sites:

Devotees often embark on pilgrimages to places associated with Saint Frances of Rome, such as her birthplace or sites where significant events in her life occurred. These pilgrimages serve as a way to deepen their connection with her spiritual legacy.

6. Patronage for Specific Needs:

Many individuals invoke Saint Frances of Rome as the patron saint for specific needs. Whether seeking assistance in matters related to family, health, or protection, believers believe in her intercessory power to bring their intentions before God.

7. Educational Initiatives:

Devotion to Saint Frances may include educational initiatives, such as the dissemination of information about her life and teachings. Books, articles, and other resources contribute to a broader understanding of her spiritual significance.

8. Iconography and Religious Art:

The saint is often depicted in religious art and iconography. Devotees may display images of Saint Frances in their homes, workplaces, or places of worship as a visual reminder of her spiritual presence.

9. Cultural Events and Celebrations:

In some regions, cultural events and celebrations are organized to honor Saint Frances of Rome. These may include processions, lectures, or exhibitions that highlight her life and impact.

Devotion to Saint Frances of Rome is a dynamic and multifaceted expression of faith, connecting believers across time and geography. Through prayer, emulation of her virtues, and commemorative practices, devotees seek to draw closer to the spiritual legacy of this revered saint.

Novenas To Saint Frances Of Rome

A novena to Saint Frances of Rome is a nine-day prayer devotion dedicated to seeking her intercession and guidance. Novenas are a longstanding tradition in the Catholic Church, involving consistent and intentional prayer over a specific period, often with the goal of seeking divine assistance, guidance, or expressing gratitude.

During a novena to Saint Frances of Rome, believers engage

in daily prayers, reflections, and supplications, seeking her intercession for various intentions. This period of focused devotion allows individuals to deepen their spiritual connection with the saint and entrust their needs to her heavenly advocacy.

The structure of a novena typically involves specific prayers or devotions repeated over the nine days, along with reflections on the life and virtues of Saint Frances. Devotees may use traditional prayers or compose personal expressions of devotion, expressing their intentions and seeking her assistance in matters such as health, family, or spiritual well-being.

Novenas to saints, including Saint Frances of Rome, are a cherished practice in the Catholic tradition, offering a dedicated and concentrated period of prayer to strengthen one's faith and seek the saint's intercession for specific needs or challenges.

Day One Novena to Saint Frances of Rome

Opening Prayer:
Dear Saint Frances of Rome, devoted servant of God and example of Christian virtue, we come before you seeking your intercession. As we embark on this novena, guide our hearts and intentions. Help us emulate your profound faith, charity, and humility.

Reflection:
On this first day, we reflect on your life, dear Saint Frances, marked by your unwavering commitment to serve God through

serving others. May your selfless acts of charity inspire us to live lives of compassion, kindness, and generosity.

Novena Prayer:
Saint Frances of Rome, you who embraced a life of humility and dedicated yourself to the service of the poor and sick, we humbly seek your intercession on this day. Please present our intentions before the throne of God.

(State your specific intentions here...)

In your profound connection with the divine, obtain for us the grace to persevere in faith, even in the face of challenges. May your example guide us towards lives of holiness and devotion.

Concluding Prayer:
O Saint Frances of Rome, who, through your virtuous life, became a beacon of light for all seeking God's love and mercy, hear our prayers. As we begin this novena, may your intercession lead us closer to the heart of God. Amen.

Closing Hymn (optional):
Consider concluding your prayer with a hymn or song dedicated to Saint Frances of Rome, expressing gratitude for her spiritual guidance and intercession.

Day Two Novena to Saint Frances of Rome

Opening Prayer:

Heavenly Father, we come before You on this second day of our novena, invoking the intercession of Saint Frances of Rome. Inspire us, O Lord, through her example of unwavering faith and tireless service to others.

Reflection:

Saint Frances, on this day, we contemplate your resilience in times of trial and your steadfast trust in God's providence. May we, too, find strength in adversity and entrust our lives to the loving care of our Heavenly Father.

Novena Prayer:

Saint Frances of Rome, renowned for your fortitude in facing life's challenges, we turn to you with confidence. Intercede on our behalf and present our intentions before the throne of grace.

(State your specific intentions here...)

Guide us, O saintly friend, in moments of difficulty, that we may emulate your trust in divine providence. Help us recognize God's hand at work in our lives and respond with faith and gratitude.

Concluding Prayer:

O Saint Frances of Rome, whose unwavering trust in God sustained you through life's trials, intercede for us. As we continue this novena, may we draw strength from your example and grow in trust and reliance on our Heavenly Father. Amen.

Closing Hymn (optional):

Consider concluding your prayer with a hymn or song dedicated to Saint Frances of Rome, expressing gratitude for her spiritual guidance and intercession.

Day Three Novena to Saint Frances of Rome

Opening Prayer:
Heavenly Father, as we gather on this third day of our novena, we seek the intercession of Saint Frances of Rome. May her virtues and holiness inspire us to draw closer to You and embrace lives of compassion and love.

Reflection:
Saint Frances, today we reflect on your ardent love for the Eucharist and your deep communion with Christ. May our hearts be opened to the transformative power of the Holy Eucharist, just as yours was during your earthly journey.

Novena Prayer:
Saint Frances of Rome, whose heart burned with love for the Eucharistic Lord, we come before you with our intentions. Present them to Christ, and ask for His grace to be poured into our lives.

(State your specific intentions here...)

Pray for us, O saintly companion, that we may approach the Eucharist with the reverence and love that characterized your spiritual life. Help us to encounter Christ in this sacrament and be transformed by His presence.

Concluding Prayer:
O Saint Frances of Rome, whose devotion to the Eucharist was a source of strength and inspiration, intercede for us. As we continue this novena, may our hearts be attuned to the presence of Christ in the Blessed Sacrament, and may we be transformed by His love. Amen.

Closing Hymn (optional):
Consider concluding your prayer with a hymn or song dedicated to Saint Frances of Rome, expressing gratitude for her spiritual guidance and intercession.

Day Four Novena to Saint Frances of Rome

Opening Prayer:
Gracious Father, on this fourth day of our novena, we lift our hearts in prayer, seeking the intercession of Saint Frances of Rome. May her life of humility and service inspire us to embrace a deeper commitment to Your will.

Reflection:
Saint Frances, today we reflect on your humility and simplicity, virtues that endeared you to God's heart. Help us, dear saint, to shed the trappings of pride and embrace a humble and straightforward life in service to others.

Novena Prayer:

Saint Frances of Rome, exemplar of humility, we entrust our intentions to your care. Present them to our Heavenly Father, and ask for the grace to cultivate humility in our lives.

(State your specific intentions here...)

Pray for us, O humble saint, that we may recognize our dependence on God and find joy in selfless service to others. Guide us in imitating your simplicity, that we may draw closer to the heart of Christ.

Concluding Prayer:

O Saint Frances of Rome, whose humility endeared you to God, intercede for us. As we progress in this novena, may the seeds of humility and simplicity take root in our hearts, leading us closer to our Heavenly Father. Amen.

Closing Hymn (optional):

Consider concluding your prayer with a hymn or song dedicated to Saint Frances of Rome, expressing gratitude for her spiritual guidance and intercession.

Day Five Novena to Saint Frances of Rome

Opening Prayer:

Heavenly Father, we gather on this fifth day of our novena, seeking the intercession of Saint Frances of Rome. May her steadfast faith and dedication to Your will be a guiding light for us on our spiritual journey.

Reflection:

Saint Frances, on this day, we contemplate your acts of charity and compassion towards the poor and sick. Inspire us to extend our hands in love and service to those in need, following your selfless example.

Novena Prayer:

Saint Frances of Rome, compassionate servant of the poor and sick, we bring our intentions before you. Present them to our Merciful Father, and ask for the grace to imitate your love for those in distress.

(State your specific intentions here...)

Pray for us, O saintly advocate, that our hearts may be filled with compassion for the less fortunate. Guide us in reaching out to those in need, and may our acts of charity be a reflection of God's boundless love.

Concluding Prayer:

O Saint Frances of Rome, whose love for the poor and sick was a reflection of Christ's compassion, intercede for us. As we continue this novena, may our hearts be open to the needs of others, and may our actions be a testament to the love of our Heavenly Father. Amen.

Closing Hymn (optional):

Consider concluding your prayer with a hymn or song dedicated to Saint Frances of Rome, expressing gratitude for her spiritual guidance and intercession.

Day Six Novena to Saint Frances of Rome

Opening Prayer:

Gracious Father, on this sixth day of our novena, we gather in prayer, seeking the intercession of Saint Frances of Rome. May her unwavering trust in Your providence inspire us to surrender our lives completely to Your divine will.

Reflection:

Saint Frances, today we reflect on your spiritual encounters and mystical experiences. May we, too, be open to the divine presence in our lives, seeking a deeper connection with God through prayer, contemplation, and an openness to divine guidance.

Novena Prayer:

Saint Frances of Rome, mystic and visionary, we bring our intentions before you. Present them to our Loving Father, and ask for the grace to be attuned to the divine whispers in our hearts.

(State your specific intentions here...)

Pray for us, O saintly mystic, that our spiritual journey may be marked by a profound awareness of God's presence. Guide us in seeking moments of contemplation and communion with the divine, just as you did.

Concluding Prayer:

O Saint Frances of Rome, whose soul was touched by mystical encounters with God, intercede for us. As we progress in this novena, may our hearts be open to the whispers of the Holy Spirit, leading us closer to the divine mysteries. Amen.

Closing Hymn (optional):
Consider concluding your prayer with a hymn or song dedicated to Saint Frances of Rome, expressing gratitude for her spiritual guidance and intercession.

Day Seven Novena to Saint Frances of Rome

Opening Prayer:
Heavenly Father, on this seventh day of our novena, we come before You, seeking the intercession of Saint Frances of Rome. May her life of faith and resilience inspire us to face challenges with unwavering trust in Your divine providence.

Reflection:
Saint Frances, today we reflect on your commitment to a life of simplicity and humility. As we strive for these virtues, help us detach from worldly distractions and embrace a humble and sincere way of living, imitating your example.

Novena Prayer:
Saint Frances of Rome, exemplar of simplicity and humility, we present our intentions before you. Lay them at the feet of our Merciful Father, and ask for the grace to live lives marked by humility and simplicity.

(State your specific intentions here...)

Pray for us, O saintly model, that our actions may reflect a humble and sincere heart. Guide us in recognizing the true source of our strength and joy—the humble and loving heart of Christ.

Concluding Prayer:
　O Saint Frances of Rome, whose life radiated simplicity and humility, intercede for us. As we continue this novena, may our hearts be transformed, embracing a life of sincere humility, and may our actions be pleasing in the eyes of our Heavenly Father. Amen.

Closing Hymn (optional):
　Consider concluding your prayer with a hymn or song dedicated to Saint Frances of Rome, expressing gratitude for her spiritual guidance and intercession.

Day Eight Novena to Saint Frances of Rome

Opening Prayer:
　Heavenly Father, as we embark on the eighth day of this novena, we seek the intercession of Saint Frances of Rome. May her legacy of selfless service and dedication to family inspire us to live virtuous lives centered on Your love.

Reflection:
　Saint Frances, today we reflect on your commitment to family

life and the responsibilities you embraced with love and devotion. Help us, O saintly companion, to prioritize our familial duties and cultivate homes filled with love, respect, and faith.

Novena Prayer:

Saint Frances of Rome, devoted spouse and mother, we entrust our intentions to your care. Present them to our Loving Father, and ask for the grace to fulfill our family responsibilities with love and dedication.

(State your specific intentions here...)

Pray for us, O saintly mother, that we may cherish and nurture our families as you did. Guide us in creating homes filled with the warmth of love and the presence of Christ.

Concluding Prayer:

O Saint Frances of Rome, whose heart was devoted to family and responsibilities, intercede for us. As we progress in this novena, may our families be sanctuaries of love and faith, and may our actions reflect Your divine love. Amen.

Closing Hymn (optional):

Consider concluding your prayer with a hymn or song dedicated to Saint Frances of Rome, expressing gratitude for her spiritual guidance and intercession.

Day Nine Novena to Saint Frances of Rome

Opening Prayer:

Gracious Father, on this ninth and final day of our novena, we gather with hearts full of gratitude for the intercession of Saint Frances of Rome. May her example continue to inspire us to live lives of faith, charity, and humility.

Reflection:

Saint Frances, today we reflect on the enduring legacy you left through the establishment of the Oblates of Mary a community devoted to serving others. As we conclude this novena, help us carry forward your mission of love and service in our own lives.

Novena Prayer:

Saint Frances of Rome, co-founder of the Oblates of Mary, we lay our intentions before you on this final day. Present them to our Heavenly Father, and ask for the grace to be instruments of His love and mercy in the world.

(State your specific intentions here...)

Pray for us, O saintly founder, that we may continue your mission of love and service. Guide us in selflessly offering our lives for the well-being of others, just as you did.

Concluding Prayer:

O Saint Frances of Rome, whose life of service continues to inspire, intercede for us. As we conclude this novena, may your example remain etched in our hearts, motivating us to live lives of profound love, faith, and service. Amen.

Closing Hymn (optional):

THE LIFE OF SAINT FRANCES OF ROME

Consider concluding your prayer with a hymn or song dedicated to Saint Frances of Rome, expressing gratitude for her spiritual guidance and intercession.

Litany To Saint Frances Of Rome

Lord, have mercy on us.
   Christ, have mercy on us.
   Lord, have mercy on us.
   Christ, hear us.
   Christ, graciously hear us.

God the Father of Heaven,
   Have mercy on us.
   God the Son, Redeemer of the world,
   Have mercy on us.
   God the Holy Spirit,
   Have mercy on us.
   Holy Trinity, one God,
   Have mercy on us.

Holy Mary, Mother of God,
   Pray for us.

Saint Frances of Rome,
   Pray for us.

Faithful servant of God,
> Pray for us.

Model of Christian virtue,
> Pray for us.

Exemplar of humility,
> Pray for us.

Dedicated spouse and mother,
> Pray for us.

Lover of the Eucharist,
> Pray for us.

Companion of angels,
> Pray for us.

Comforter of the sick and poor,
> Pray for us.

Patroness of widows,
> Pray for us.

Guide in family life,
> Pray for us.

Founder of the Oblates of Mary,
> Pray for us.

Joyful in obedience,
> Pray for us.

Patient in suffering,
> Pray for us.

Generous in charity,
> Pray for us.

Discerner of God's will,
> Pray for us.

Faithful in prayer,
> Pray for us.

Model of marital love,
Pray for us.
Consoler of the afflicted,
Pray for us.
Friend of the poor,
Pray for us.

Lover of simplicity,
Pray for us.
Humble in heart,
Pray for us.
Mystic in contemplation,
Pray for us.
Bearer of Christ's wounds in spirit,
Pray for us.
Intercessor for the needy,
Pray for us.
Example of holiness,
Pray for us.

Lamb of God, who takes away the sins of the world,
Have mercy on us.

Lamb of God, who takes away the sins of the world,
Graciously hear us, O Lord.

Lamb of God, who takes away the sins of the world,
Have mercy on us.

Pray for us, Saint Frances of Rome,
That we may be made worthy of the promises of Christ.

Let us pray:

O God, who adorned Saint Frances of Rome with the virtues of obedience, humility, and charity, grant, through her intercession, that, freed from earthly attachments, we may follow Christ in faith and love. Through our Lord Jesus Christ, your Son, who lives and reigns with you in the unity of the Holy Spirit, one God, forever and ever. Amen.

Additional Prayers To Saint Frances Of Rome

Prayer for Guidance in Family Life:

Saint Frances of Rome, devoted spouse and mother, you navigated the responsibilities of family life with unwavering faith and love. Intercede for us as we face the challenges of our own families. Obtain for us the grace to prioritize love, understanding, and faith within our homes. May your example guide us in fostering unity and joy in our families, just as you did in yours. Amen.

Prayer for Charity and Compassion:

Saint Frances of Rome, compassionate friend of the poor and sick, teach us the essence of true charity. Inspire within us a selfless love for those in need, and guide us to extend our hands in compassion. May your legacy of charitable deeds be a beacon, leading us to recognize the face of Christ in those who suffer.

Through your intercession, help us cultivate a generous and merciful heart. Amen.

Prayer for Humility and Simplicity:
O Saint Frances of Rome, whose life radiated with humility and simplicity, intercede for us in our journey towards these virtues. Help us cast aside the distractions of worldly pursuits and embrace a life marked by humility and sincerity. May your example guide us to recognize the beauty in simplicity and find joy in humble service. Through your intercession, may we grow in true Christian humility. Amen.

Prayer for Those Facing Illness:
Saint Frances of Rome, compassionate comforter of the sick, we turn to you on behalf of those facing illness. Intercede for them before our Heavenly Father, that they may find strength, solace, and healing. May your example of caring for the sick inspire us to extend our hands in love to those in need. Through your prayers, may the suffering find relief and the sick be restored to health. Amen.

Prayer for Discernment of God's Will:
Saint Frances of Rome, discerning servant of God, guide us in discerning His will in our lives. Obtain for us the wisdom to recognize His plan and the courage to follow it with steadfast faith. May your life, marked by obedience and trust, inspire us to surrender our hearts completely to the divine will. Through your intercession, may we navigate life's decisions with grace

and fidelity to God's purpose. Amen.

Concluding Prayers To Saint Frances Of Rome

O Saint Frances of Rome, shining example of faith and virtue, we humbly thank you for your intercession and guidance throughout this time of prayer. As we conclude our devotion, may your heavenly influence continue to inspire and lead us on the path of holiness. Help us to live lives of charity, humility, and unwavering trust in God's providence. Through your prayers, may we draw closer to Christ and reflect His love in our daily actions. Amen.

Saint Frances of Rome, faithful servant of God, as we conclude this time of prayer and reflection, we express our gratitude for your intercession and the inspiration drawn from your holy life. May the virtues you embodied humility, charity, and unwavering faith continue to shape our hearts and actions. Through your prayers, may we be strengthened in our journey of faith and find courage to live out the Gospel in our daily lives. Amen.

O Saint Frances of Rome, devoted spouse, mother, and servant of the poor, as we conclude this novena, we thank you for your intercession and the lessons drawn from your life. May your example encourage us to live lives of selfless love and service to others. Through your prayers, may we be granted the grace to face life's challenges with unwavering faith and to walk in the footsteps of Christ. Amen.

10

Conclusion

In conclusion, the life of Saint Frances of Rome unfolds as a luminous tapestry woven with threads of faith, compassion, and unwavering dedication to God. As we traverse the pages of her extraordinary journey, we witness a woman whose existence transcended the ordinary, leaving an indelible mark on the annals of Christian history.

Frances' birth into a noble Roman family set the stage for a life that would be anything but conventional. From her early years marked by spiritual inclinations to the profound spiritual awakening she experienced, we see the gradual unfolding of a soul deeply attuned to the divine. Her upbringing and education, though rooted in the societal norms of her time, became the fertile ground for the seeds of holiness that would later blossom.

The pivotal moment of her arranged marriage to Lorenzo Ponziani, a union initially orchestrated by her parents, proved instrumental in her spiritual journey. Far from resisting this arrangement, Frances embraced her role as a wife and mother with an unwavering commitment to God's will. Her family life became a testament to the transformative power of faith, where she navigated the complexities of marriage and motherhood with grace and love.

Frances' spiritual odyssey took a profound turn with her founding of the Oblates of Mary a community dedicated to serving the poor and sick. The establishment of this lay order was a radical departure from societal norms, reflecting her deep conviction that true holiness is found in humble service to others. The subsequent chapters of her life were painted with strokes of charity, as she dedicated herself to the alleviation of suffering and the pursuit of justice.

A recurring theme in Saint Frances' narrative is her embrace of a simple lifestyle. Whether in the care of her family or her devotion to the impoverished, she exemplified the beauty found in detachment from material pursuits. Her personal sacrifices for others were not merely acts of generosity but profound expressions of her profound love for Christ and her fellow human beings.

The significance of the Eucharist in her life cannot be overstated. It was in the reception of the Holy Communion that Frances found strength, solace, and communion with Christ. The Eucharist was the wellspring from which she drew the fortitude to face life's challenges and the inspiration to extend love and compassion to those in need.

Her practices and rituals were not mere formalities but expressions of a deep and abiding faith. From her reported miracles to mystical encounters and visions, the supernatural dimensions of her life serve as a testament to the profound connection she shared with the divine. The canonization and declaration of sainthood by Pope Paul V in 1608 further affirmed the sanctity of her life.

As we reflect on the continued influence and commemoration of Saint Frances of Rome, her legacy is not confined to historical accounts or religious rituals. It is a living testament that resonates in the hearts of those who, inspired by her example, strive for lives of compassion, humility, and faith. The devotion to Saint Frances of Rome, as seen in liturgical prayers and novenas, is a vibrant expression of the enduring impact of her spiritual journey.

In conclusion, the life of Saint Frances of Rome beckons us to embark on our own spiritual odyssey a journey marked by faith, love, and service to others. Through the pages of this book, we have encountered a woman whose life transcended the constraints of her time, leaving an indelible imprint on the collective consciousness of believers. As we close this chapter, may the radiant example of Saint Frances of Rome continue to illuminate our paths, inspiring us to lead lives that resonate with the eternal melody of divine love.